35-DAY
Bible Study
for YOUNG
BLACK MEN

Inell Williams

Daily Scripture Readings, Affirmations & Prompts to Guide Black Teenage Guys to Manhood

35-DAY
Bible Study
for YOUNG
BLACK MEN

_____

_____

Copyright © 2023 Inell Williams.
All rights reserved. No part of this book may be reproduced, stored in a retrieval system, or transmitted in any form or by any means, electronic, mechanical, photocopying, recording, or otherwise, without prior written permission of the copyright owner.

FROM THE PUBLISHER:

Thank you for purchasing 35-Day Bible Study for Young Black Men and supporting a small, black-owned business!

This book was created with the guidance and input of various strong Black men of God. Right now there is an unmet need for more spiritual guidance for Black male youth. We hope that this book could be a useful tool for helping them reach their full potential as followers of Christ and as young men.

We encourage you to leave a rating or review on Amazon; it would be greatly appreciated. Is there anything you'd like to see improved? What verses did you enjoy most? Let us know what you think!

-Inell Williams

TABLE OF CONTENTS

Introduction 5
Day 1: Provider 6
Day 2: Responsibility 8
Day 3: Leader 10
Day 4: Bad Company 12
Day 5: Honesty 14
Day 6: Control My Emotions 16
Day 7: Gratitude 18
Day 8: Protector 20
Day 9: Work Ethic 22
Day 10: Character 24
Day 11: Wisdom 26
Day 12: Mind & Body 28
Day 13: Finances 30
Day 14: Bearing My Cross 32
Day 15: Strength 34
Day 16: Temptation 36
Day 17: Authority 38
Day 18: Empathy 40
Day 19: Faithful 42
Day 20: Discipline 44
Day 21: Black King 46
Day 22: Mentor/ Father Figure 48
Day 23: Girls 50
Day 24: Honor 52
Day 25: Confidence 54
Day 26: Manhood 56
Day 27: Respect 58
Day 28: Perseverance 60
Day 29: Reputation 62
Day 30: Race 64
Day 31: Ambition 66
Day 32: Courage 68
Day 33: Pray More 70
Day 34: Masculinity 72
Day 35: No Perfect Man 74

INTRODUCTION

This Bible study takes you on a 35-day journey of spiritual enrichment. It provides you a quick and convenient way to get into the habit of devoting time to God.

All verses are quoted from the World English Bible (WEB). Below the explanation of scripture, a couple of lines are provided to optionally jot down any thoughts that spring to mind. Perhaps the verse or explanation reminds you of something, or maybe you want to look up and write down another verse that is cited. Or you can jot down the meaning of a word that is new to you.

On the right-hand side of this book, each Bible verse is accompanied by an affirmation and at least two prompts to fortify your understanding, or to help you better remember the scriptures. Space is provided for brief answers.

What you'll need for this Bible study:

- a pencil or pen
- 10 minutes each day
- a heart and mind ready to connect with God

DAY 1: PROVIDER

1 TIMOTHY 5:8

"But if anyone doesn't provide for his own, and especially his own household, he has denied the faith, and is worse than an unbeliever."

One of a man's most important responsibilities is to be a provider. Since the beginning of human history, women, children and other vulnerable members of society have looked to men to provide resources, and thereby take care of everyone. A man who doesn't provide is so offensive to God that he is deemed worse than an infidel, or one who does not believe in Him. The average young, healthy man has biological advantages given to him by God, like greater strength (1 Peter 3:7). This makes it easier for him to gather resources compared to women, the very young, and the very old. This greater power, bestowed upon you by God, comes with a greater responsibility to those who depend on you as a man in your household, relationships, and community.

My thoughts/ notes:

_____

_____

As a young Black man, I am a provider. God's divine hand guides me into providing for those in my life now and in the future.

Across the world men provide financially for women and children and their community. But what else do men provide?

_____

_____

_____

Name two examples of Black men you admire. How do they provide for their loved ones? They can be someone you know or know of.

_____

_____

_____

DAY 2: RESPONSIBILITY

1 CORINTHIANS 13:11

"When I was a child, I spoke as a child, I felt as a child, I thought as a child. Now that I have become a man, I have put away childish things."

As a young man, you are at an exciting point in your life where you're transitioning from boyhood to manhood. This is where you start finding your own path in the world. Picture someone who has developed a reputation for being thoughtful about how their actions affect them. They embrace self-discipline and strive to be someone who people can rely on. By doing this, they become someone who people can trust and have faith in. As a young man, you have a responsibility to God to fulfill certain manly duties that He expects of you. It is a key part of your place in this world. So embrace the journey of maturing, because through responsibilities you will find true fulfillment, gain God's approval, and make a positive impact on the world as a man.

My thoughts/ notes:

_____

_____

Responsibility is the core of who I am as a young man of God. Christ and the Bible give me the wisdom to know how to honor God through my masculine duties.

How does taking on responsibilities lead to more fulfillment as a man, especially as a man of Christ?

_____

_____

_____

We all fall short of the perfect model that is Christ. What is one thing in your life you could be more responsible about? How can you improve in that area?

_____

_____

_____

DAY 3: LEADER

1 TIMOTHY 3:2-3

"...The overseer therefore must be without reproach, the husband of one wife, temperate, sensible, modest, hospitable, good at teaching; not a drinker, not violent, not greedy for money..."

What is a leader? In simple terms, it's someone who takes on more responsibilities than others to make things run smoothly. Imagine you're in a group project with five people, and there is no leader. Without one, it's harder for your group to be organized and to meet deadlines. Because of this, all group members are worried and stressed. But what if someone steps up to the plate and decides to lead? They divide the group tasks for everyone, make the major decisions and hold people accountable. Now everyone is productive and less worried. Everything's organized and completed thanks to the leader. This is what good leaders do: they give everyone a sense of direction and safety.

My thoughts/ notes:

_____

_____

As a young man God calls upon me to be a future leader. I can serve the Almighty by serving others with masculine guidance and leadership.

In this verse, "overseer" is another word for leader. Overall, how should an overseer act to be a good leader?

_____

_____

_____

As Christians, it is expected that our actions are done with love (1 Corinthians 16:14). How can you lead with love?

_____

_____

_____

DAY 4: BAD COMPANY

1 TIMOTHY 4:12

"Do not be deceived: 'Bad company ruins good morals'."

Have you ever felt self-conscious for being different in some way from the people around you? Maybe you know what it's like to be afraid to have a different opinion, or to do something that you don't believe in or don't think is good. In situations like these always remember that the right people in life will support you if you try to take a more noble, godly path. If you are on a journey to be a saved young man, you must have the courage to think for yourself and stay on the right path, even if it's unpopular. Stick with people who want to become wise in God with you, and don't hang around those who may lead you or themselves on the path to destruction (Proverbs 13:20). You can listen to others' opinions - knowing that people can always teach you something new - but at the end of the day your godly values come first. Always have the strength to make that clear to people.

My thoughts/ notes:

_____

_____

I am strong enough to overcome peer pressure because I know none is greater than God. The Almighty's opinions matter more than anyone else's.

Can you remember an example of a time you felt pressured to follow someone else's path rather than your own? Briefly describe that here.

_____
_____
_____

You are called to not associate yourself with that which is ungodly. See 1 Corinthians 5:11 for a few examples of this. Are there other examples of ungodliness in a friend you can think of?

_____
_____
_____

DAY 5: HONESTY

PROVERBS 12:22

"Lying lips are an abomination to Yahweh, but those who do the truth are his delight."

A man is only as good as his word, as the saying goes. But we have all been tempted to lie or deceive to avoid repercussions. What are the long-term consequences of this? Imagine someone who goes about life lying to get their way. When others catch them lying repeatedly, they put distance between them. The liar sees their relationships and opportunities falling apart around them, and experiences the sharp pain of regret. Your uprightness is endangered by lies. Choosing to speak the truth and act with integrity builds a strong foundation for your life in the name of the Almighty. And if you are trying to get closer to Christ, having lies on your tongue will weigh heavily on your conscience. It is easier to rest at night knowing that you are not going to be caught in a lie (Hebrews 13:18).

My thoughts/ notes:

_____

_____

As a disciple of Christ, I strive towards honesty and uprightness. I honor my Lord by living with integrity.

We're all guilty of being "double-minded" sometimes - meaning we have a certain moral standard, but our actions don't always live up to it. Do you have an example of this in your life?

_____

_____

_____

Honesty can be applied not only to other people, but to ourselves. What are two ways you can be more honest with yourself to become a better Christian?

_____

_____

_____

DAY 6: CONTROL MY EMOTIONS

PROVERBS 16:32

"One who is slow to anger is better than the mighty; one who rules his spirit, than he who takes a city."

Like a mighty warrior who conquers his own impulses, you have the ability to rise above strong emotions. A careful man truly tries his best to control his emotions and actions in challenging situations. This is a sign of great wisdom and strength. When you are provoked or face adversity, resist the urge to respond with aggression or recklessness. Take a deep breath and refuse to engage. By allowing yourself to be provoked, you put the provoking person first. Instead, put yourself first. Think about how a strong reaction from you could negatively affect you in the future. A man who has no restraint, who cannot control himself, is like an unprotected city, vulnerable to attacks from the outside (Proverbs 25:28). As a strong, young Black man, you are not ruled by emotions, no: they are ruled by you.

My thoughts/ notes:

_____

_____

I am human so I am not perfect, but with the Holy Spirit's guidance I can control my emotions. Christ teaches me how to be more and more mindful each day.

Throughout time and through many cultures manliness is associated with emotional restraint. Why do you think that is?

_____

_____

_____

Have you experienced losing control of your emotions before? Briefly describe that experience. What were the results of that?

_____

_____

_____

DAY 7: GRATITUDE

PSALM 118:24

"This is the day that Yahweh has made. We will rejoice and be glad in it!"

Choosing to be thankful everyday is a very good tool to carry with you throughout your life. Reminding yourself to have gratitude gives glory to God as it means you are appreciating what He has given you. It helps you cultivate a positive attitude, which is useful, because it makes taking on hard tasks less daunting. When the going gets tough, you can tell God: Lord, it's hard right now, but I thank you for taking me this far. I know you will take me even further.

With the guidance of the Holy Spirit learn to seize each day as a precious gift from Christ. When you come across smaller upsets throughout your day, let them go. Let them have little effect on the bigger picture. Focus on your blessings and more will come.

My thoughts/ notes:

_____

_____

I appreciate all that God provides for me, even during hard times. I humbly accept His provisions and the opportunities He gives me.

How can being grateful make you a stronger man? How can it make you a successful man?

_____
_____
_____

Name three things that you are thankful for.

_____
_____
_____

DAY 8: PROTECTOR

GENESIS 2:15

"Yahweh God took the man, and put him into the garden of Eden to cultivate and keep it."

In this context the word "keep" means guard or protect. This meaning of keep is also used when Cain says "Am I my brother's keeper?" in Genesis 4:9, meaning guardian or protector. Just as the first man on Earth protected Eden, men today all over the world are tasked with the duty of being protectors. What do men keep in particular? They protect women, children, the old, the ill, their family and loved ones. They guard their community and especially their home from harm. Being understanding of others' vulnerability to harm is a part of a man's protective instincts. An example of this is found in 1 Peter 3:7 when men are told to honor women as the weaker vessel. This refers to looking out for and showing respect towards those who may have less means of protecting themselves.

My thoughts/ notes:

_____

_____

I walk in the footsteps of the Lord when I protect and keep those around me.

Are there any ways besides physical means that men can protect others?

_____

_____

_____

Who do you feel protective of in your life?

_____

_____

_____

DAY 9: WORK ETHIC

GENESIS 3:17-19

"...The ground is cursed for your sake. You will eat from it with much labor all the days of your life... You will eat bread by the sweat of your face until you return to the ground..."

After eating the forbidden fruit, Adam and Eve received two separate punishments from God. The punishment given to Adam was that, unlike in Eden, food would no longer be readily available. It would be Adam's responsibility to work hard if he wants to eat. A good work ethic can open countless doors. Being able to put your head down and hustle is a valuable skill to learn. It gives you the ability to create opportunities for yourself to succeed. It is good to work hard and earnestly, especially for yourself and for the Lord (Colossians 3:23), as you will find that achieving through the sweat of your brow is rewarding on a deep level. Pursuit of hard work ultimately helps men reach their potential for greatness.

My thoughts/ notes:

_____

_____

I get closer and closer towards my full potential, bestowed upon my future by God, the more I work. He has wondrous plans in store for me.

Name one thing that you would like to see yourself do within the next five to ten years:

_____

Imagine what it would be like to have God fulfill this. What would that look like? What positive results can you expect?

_____

_____

_____

_____

_____

What is at least one thing you have to do to accomplish this goal?

_____

DAY 10: CHARACTER

PROVERBS 10:9

"He who walks blamelessly walks surely, but he who perverts his ways will be found out."

What if you were in a situation where you found a lost wallet on the street? Most would be tempted to keep the money for themselves. But what if you returned the wallet to it's rightful owner? God would see this and bestow blessings upon you. He notices when we've chosen the path of righteousness (Isaiah 33:15-17). What's important to note is that being righteous doesn't mean that you are never tempted by Satan. It means that though you felt the devil's pull, you still chose to do the right thing. The good Lord gives us free will to develop our character as much or as little as we all please (Galatians 5:13). We all can either strive to move closer to Christ, closer to His way of being, or move away from Him. How close or far away you want to be from Christ reflects upon your character in the eyes of God.

My thoughts/ notes:

_____

_____

I am upright, and I am careful. I am virtuous and godly. I embrace God to use me in His righteous plans for my life.

List some good character traits that Lord Jesus is known for.

_____

_____

_____

Name at least one man or young man in your life who is of good character. What do you admire about their character?

_____

_____

_____

DAY 11: WISDOM

PROVERBS 24:5-6

"A wise man has great power; and a knowledgeable man increases strength; for by wise guidance you wage your war; and victory is in many advisors."

Wisdom is a reliable shield that protects you from bad mistakes. It acts as a friend in times of uncertainty. Imagine you are trying to make a big decision in your life. Maybe you're trying to choose a life partner or make an important financial decision. For something as important as these, don't assume that you know all. Instead of relying just on your instincts or limited understanding, take the time to research, ask questions, and gather more information (Proverbs 12:15). Only take advice from those who make life choices that yield good results and are of God. Having wisdom doesn't only help you, it can serve the people around you. When you display sound judgement, others will respect your thoughts and seek out your guidance and leadership.

My thoughts/ notes:

_____

_____

Lord, there are no limits to the wisdom that you can impart to me. Fill me with your divine knowledge. Give me the drive to increase my wisdom always.

What is one thing that you want to become more wise about in your life? Let God know what that is.

_____

_____

_____

Who is a man whom you consider wise? What makes them wise?

_____

_____

_____

DAY 12: MIND & BODY

1 CORINTHIANS 6:19

"Or don't you know that your body is a temple of the Holy Spirit who is in you, whom you have from God? You are not your own..."

Your body belongs to God. As such, consider it sacred and invaluable. It shows great respect to God to give glory to this vessel that He gifted you. In other words, self-care is next to godliness. How might your connection with the Almighty suffer if you don't take care of yourself? Sometimes we all struggle with keeping our room clean and orderly. The Lord knows you're not perfect, but He appreciates when you try to hold yourself to a certain standard. Prioritize your physical and mental well-being in your sleep, eating habits, and avoiding harmful substances. Also, keeping fit will help you have a masculine confidence in yourself. By treating your body with respect and care, you honor both yourself and the divine essence within you.

My thoughts/ notes:

_____

_____

I honor this body that the Lord has gifted me. My body is a temple worth cherishing.

What are at least two things you can do to improve your self-care?

_____

_____

_____

How would these improvements enhance your life?

_____

_____

_____

DAY 13: FINANCES

LUKE 14:28

"For which of you, desiring to build a tower, doesn't first sit down and count the cost, to see if he has enough to complete it?"

It is important to practice handling money with careful planning and consideration. Thinking about the consequences of your financial choices will help you reach any goals you have with money. Men are called by the Almighty God to be providers, leaders of their households, and self-reliant. To fulfill these godly roles, learning how to handle money is necessary. Think about your financial goals and aspirations. What steps should you take to accomplish them? Keeping track of how much money you're bringing in and how much you're spending is a good and simple place to start. By planning for your financial future you can build a strong foundation for yourself and for those who may depend on you, God willing.

My thoughts/ notes:

_____

_____

God show me the way to budgeting discipline and financial peace. Prosperity and financial freedom are blessings that are within my reach.

YouTube finance channels can be great for learning finance. A good example is Two Cents. Search topics like "how to build good credit" or "how much money to save" and see what other YT channels pop up. Write down at least one that appeals to you.

_____
_____
_____

Two of the deadly sins - envy and gluttony - often make people overspend. With Christ's help, how can you keep yourself from overspending?

_____
_____
_____

DAY 14: BEARING MY CROSS

GALATIANS 6:5

"For each man will bear his own burden."

Being a man isn't easy. Being a Black man comes with even more challenges. But you can trust in the Lord that He has made you strong enough to handle this, since you have the power to shape your own destiny through the choices you make. Depending on the path you choose, your cross can become heavier or lighter. Think about a man who sets goals, works hard, and rises above challenges in his career. In the end he sees the positive outcomes of his hard work. But if he neglects his responsibilities or engages in harmful acts, he experiences negative consequences. As a man you will have to soldier on for yourself and for others, and often alone. Whatever obstacles you may go through in life, just know that you can always seek out the Lord for His strength (1 Chronicles 16:11). Your trials will build character. It's all a part of God's plan to make you a stronger man.

My thoughts/ notes:

_____

_____

My God is a great God. None is more glorious than Him. He is a pillar of strength that I can lean on in rough times so that I, too, can be a pillar of strength.

What kinds of challenges might you expect to encounter as a Black man, or as a man?

_____

_____

_____

Recall one obstacle that you had to overcome recently, big or small. Write a brief prayer thanking the Lord for getting you through it.

_____

_____

_____

DAY 15: STRENGTH

PHILIPPIANS 4:13

"I can do all things through Christ, who strengthens me."

Having a strong body, mind and spirit is essential for being a godly provider, protector and leader. Ask yourself: how can I become better physically, mentally, and emotionally? How can I challenge myself? Your masculinity thrives in challenge. It's better to proactively choose to take on a challenge before life even throws another one your way. This gives you a sense of control and agency. Strive to be a pillar of strength, to be disagreeable when necessary, and use your strength to defend those who cannot defend themselves. With Christ you have the power and resilience to overcome any challenges that come your way. He is like a beacon of light in the night sky, shepherding us towards comfort in trying times. This is why the Lord tells us to fear not (Isaiah 41:10). You can lean on Jesus in all of His divine strength and wisdom to see you through the other side.

My thoughts/ notes:

_____

_____

The Holy Spirit within me can replenish my strength again and again. All I must do is put my faith in Christ.

Who is the strongest man you know or know of? What makes him strong?

_____
_____
_____

What is one thing you can do to become stronger whether mentally, emotionally or physically? Ask the Lord for it.

_____
_____
_____

DAY 16: TEMPTATION

MATTHEW 26:41

"Watch and pray, that you don't enter into temptation. The spirit indeed is willing, but the flesh is weak."

We all are sometimes tempted to sin or not live up to our full potential in some way. Like a soldier remains alert on the battlefield, you must be attentive to temptations that may arise in your own life. Always pray for guidance from God above. Consider a situation where you have the opportunity to do something that goes against your values. When something threatens to steer you off of your path - whether that be procrastination, girls, a less than ideal friend - take a pause and ask yourself, what might Jesus do? In moments of vulnerability or peer pressure, it's so easy to let your guard down and succumb to temptation. You will have a whole life ahead of you where you will be faced with tough choices, so you will have to practice being vigilant and steadfast in your goals and beliefs.

My thoughts/ notes:

_____

_____

Lord I am human, so I am tempted. But no mountain is too large for you to overcome. You can help me overcome any temptation.

The seven deadly sins are lust, gluttony, greed, laziness, wrath, envy, and pride. Of these, which two sins do you struggle with most?

_____

_____

_____

What are some things you can do to avoid or overcome these sins?

_____

_____

_____

DAY 17: AUTHORITY

COLOSSIANS 3:12-13

"But I would have you know that the head of every man is Christ, and the head of the woman is man, and the head of Christ is God."

There is a divine hierarchy of love and care: Man takes care of woman, woman takes care of child, and God takes care of everyone. This chain of care also comes with a chain of authority. With authority comes certain rights, and certain duties. Throughout your life you may find yourself in positions of authority: at work, school, with family, etc. The rights and respect that comes with this authority is earned. And these rights always come with responsibilities. When you fulfill your duties as a man, you show people that they can rely on you. They can trust and look up to you, because they feel safe with you. Show other men and women that you can be a good leader, and they will follow your lead, and accept your authority.

My thoughts/ notes:

_____

_____

With the help of Christ and the Holy Spirit within me I can fully embrace the role of leadership and responsibility that God expects of men.

What responsibilities do you think a man holds as the head of the relationship with his woman?

_____

_____

_____

We've all been lead by a higher authority before, whether that is a teacher, parent, older sibling, etc. What kinds of traits have you liked most about people in positions of authority in your life?

_____

_____

_____

DAY 18: EMPATHY

LUKE 10:33-34

"...When he saw him, he was moved with compassion, came to him, and bound up his wounds, pouring on oil and wine. He set him on his own animal, brought him to an inn, and took care of him."

This is a part of the Parable of the Good Samaritan. Here a man was beaten and left for dead. A kind stranger makes sure that the man is okay. Men like this, who cultivate a spirit of empathy and compassion towards people, are admired and valued by others. The meek and long-suffering are considered favored by God (Matthew 5:5), and those who defend them can also be considered blessed. Empathy is also an important quality to have for leadership. The best leaders have the ability to put themselves in the shoes of the people who follow them. This makes their leadership style more democratic, and helps them be more well-informed in their decision-making.

My thoughts/ notes:

As I was made in God's image, I was given the ability to be empathetic. My empathy pales in comparison to the Lord's, but He shows me the meaning of compassion and mercy.

Briefly recall a time when someone showed you empathy.

_____
_____
_____

God used that person to comfort or encourage you. Write a prayer for them.

_____
_____
_____

DAY 19: FAITHFUL

REVELATION 2:10

"...Behold, the devil is about to throw some of you into prison, that you may be tested; and you will have oppression for ten days. Be faithful to death, and I will give you the crown of life."

Maintaining your belief in Christ ensures that when your time comes you will have a deathless death. Eternal life awaits those who remain loyal to the Almighty. So stand firm in your beliefs and you will be heavily rewarded in the afterlife. Unwavering faith in God is a sign of great strength and character. If faith threatens to escape you, think of the early believers mentioned in the book of Revelation. They remained faithful in their convictions despite all of the trials and pressures around them. By staying true to your beliefs and relying on your relationship with God, you can persevere and overcome great obstacles. After all, there is no greater reward than to reside at God's side in His kingdom for all eternity!

My thoughts/ notes:

_____

_____

Faith makes me a stronger man. I am made better each day because of the influence Christ has in my life.

When was the last time you struggled with faith? What caused this?

_____

_____

_____

The Bible tells us that without faith God cannot be pleased (Hebrews 11:6). Write a brief prayer telling Him you accept Him with all of your heart and soul.

_____

_____

_____

DAY 20: DISCIPLINE

HEBREWS 12:11

"All chastening seems for the present to be not joyous but grievous; yet afterward it yields the peaceful fruit of righteousness to those who have been trained by it."

Being conscientious (disciplined) is a huge advantage for you in life. This is true whether you are self-disciplined or were taught discipline from someone else. The work of the devil has to fight hard to puncture the wall of the disciplined man. Discipline is like a big moat and fortress that keeps out evil. A strong and godly man practices not to indulge in sin. He isn't perfect but maintains high standards for himself out of self-respect and respect for the Savior. This is hard work of course, but the Bible reminds us that we reap what we sow (2 Corinthians 9:6). Thus putting extra effort to practice delaying gratification will yield you benefits in the long run. It will also make you an admirable, reliable, and godly man that others can depend upon and look up to.

My thoughts/ notes:

As a disciple of Christ, I strive to be disciplined to please my Lord and to meet my potential.

Discipline is a form of love, whether it comes from yourself or someone else. Name someone in your life who helps you be more disciplined.

_____

_____

_____

What two specific things you can do to become more disciplined?

_____

_____

_____

DAY 21: BLACK KING

2 KINGS 19:9

"When he heard it said of Tirhakah king of Ethiopia, "Behold, he has come out to fight against you, he sent messengers again to Hezekiah..."

Taharqa was a Sudanese king of Kush (Ethiopia/ Nubia). He became Pharaoh of Egypt in 690 B.C. He's mentioned twice in the Bible - in 2 Kings and Isaiah - as "Tirhakah". Taharqa accomplished great feats during his nearly thirty-year reign, like successfully reuniting the land, and overseeing the creation of the largest pyramid ever built in Nubia. He supported many projects in the arts, including architectural and religious proposals. His time as both King and Pharaoh saw a period of prosperity and abundance for Egypt and Kush. His parents, being royalty themselves, raised and disciplined Taharqa and his brother so that they would be prepared to take on the responsibilities that come with being a successful ruler.

My thoughts/ notes:

_____

_____

I aspire to follow the example set by the King of kings Christ Himself. Humanity has never seen a greater king than Jesus.

What do you think are some qualities that Tirhakah had to have to become a king? What did he need to be successful as King?

_____

_____

_____

What qualities would make a king holy in the eyes of God?

_____

_____

_____

DAY 22: MENTOR/ FATHER FIGURE

MATTHEW 23:9

"Call no man on the earth your father, for one is your Father, he who is in heaven."

All over the world there are initiation rituals into manhood. These are a rite of passage to say goodbye to boyhood and step fully into your masculinity. Here young men develop into strong, prepared men with the guidance of other men, usually older, wiser ones. The best male mentors and role models in these initiations submit to the will of God. They recognize that while they strive to be a good model, the world has known no greater father than God. They know Christ is the example. A man among men, King of Kings and Lord of Lords, they accept Him as the ultimate man. A good mentor may take you under their wing and share knowledge and life experiences with you. They may offer a listening ear and serve as a source of encouragement, guiding you into your potential for greatness as a man.

My thoughts/ notes:

_____

_____

I am shapeable, moldable, and teachable. God the Father is the ultimate father and mentor to all men.

What are some fatherly traits that our glorious God has?

_____

_____

_____

Do you know or know of some men with these same traits? Write their names.

_____

_____

_____

DAY 23: GIRLS

PROVERBS 31:30

"Charm is deceitful, and beauty is vain; but a woman who fears Yahweh, she shall be praised."

One way the biblical relationship between man and woman can be described is this: the man is the shell, and the woman is the pearl inside the shell. The woman is covered, protected by her man and treated as something precious. She is a part of him, like Eve was a part of Adam (Genesis 2:23). Good women can sometimes be hard to come across, but when you do find them, know that they are worth so much in the eyes of the Lord (Proverbs 31:10). When God tells you it's time to find a partner, remember that water seeks its own level. Not everyone can recognize or cherish a good thing, but a good woman will appreciate a good man, and vice versa. So strive to be a good man if you want a good woman. Strive to be god-fearing so the women you attract are god-fearing as well.

My thoughts/ notes:

_____

_____

I trust that God has or will send me the right partner at the right time according to His plan.

Eve was physically a part of Adam, but what does it mean to really be a part of someone? What does it mean to become one with your partner?

_____

_____

_____

List some godly traits that someone can bring to make a relationship more holy.

_____

_____

_____

DAY 24: HONOR

PROVERBS 21:21

"He who follows after righteousness and kindness finds life, righteousness, and honor."

Living a life of honor and integrity is essential in your walk with Christ. Most male sub-cultures around the world have a tradition of a masculine code of behavior and principles. Even old school gangsters swore an oath towards an honor code. Those who went against this code faced severe consequences. Why do men strive to hold themselves and other men to high standards? To have high status in their group, and to keep order. Among god-fearing men the ultimate status symbol is to associate yourself only with that which is godly. In a social circle that values high morals, men admire other men who stay true to their religious principles. Thus it is useful to try and surround yourself with other guys who think it is cool to strive to be Christ-like. You can hold each other to high standards of righteousness.

My thoughts/ notes:

As a Christian my honor code follows God's law. I am not moved by changing earthly standards of morality.

Daniel and David are good examples of men of the Bible who are known for their integrity. Name one man whom you know of or know personally who is honorable. What makes them honorable?

_____

_____

_____

Choosing to be honorable means learning to live with some discomfort. Briefly name one example of this in your own life.

_____

_____

_____

DAY 25: CONFIDENCE

HEBREWS 10:35-36

"Therefore don't throw away your boldness, which has a great reward. For you need endurance so that, having done the will of God, you may receive the promise."

Picture yourself at the entrance of a dark cave. There's a close friend or loved one in there and they need help. You have to enter, but fear grips your heart and makes you pause. What can you do? Call upon God to watch over you. He is always with you wherever you go (Joshua 1:9) so ask Him to give you strength. The duties that men have unto others and themselves are often not easy. Being the brave and courageous one is difficult in some situations. But you must trust that as a young man God made you strong enough to carry out His will (Philippians 4:13). With the help of Christ you can overcome any obstacle and reach your aspirations, God willing. Only He will give you the confidence needed to overcome and march on.

My thoughts/ notes:

_____

_____

I am brave. I am confident. I am capable of becoming the man that God wants me to be.

What are some benefits to you as a young man from building or maintaining your confidence?

_____

_____

_____

Write a brief prayer that you can use for when you need courage. Keeping it short and making it rhyme can help you remember it better.

_____

_____

_____

DAY 26: MANHOOD

EPHESIANS 4:13

"...Until we all attain to the unity of the faith and of the knowledge of the Son of God, to a full grown man, to the measure of the stature of the fullness of Christ..."

Men are important. They are needed to lead, provide and protect. When they are not there, their absence is felt. There is less order, less safety, and society falls into chaos. Men have two main powers that affect society in a huge way: they can create, or they can destroy. So long as they are creating and fostering positivity, they provide immeasurable value to society as a whole. Imagine a place where all of the men are gone, or where the good men leave and bad, ungodly men reign. What would Heaven think peering down on this lost and godless place, with few godly men to bring order? It is important for men to be guided to realize their potential in the full likeness of Christ. This helps them use their power for good, especially for the good of society.

My thoughts/ notes:

As an individual young man, I accept the responsibility that God has given me and other men to lead myself and society down a godly path.

What are some positive things that God has helped men do for society?

_____

_____

_____

What are some negatives that occur when men as a collective choose not to honor God's will for society? Give some specific examples.

_____

_____

_____

DAY 27: RESPECT

2 TIMOTHY 3:14-15

"Honor all men. Love the brotherhood. Fear God. Honor the king."

Respect comes in different forms. Some forms are earned, like through old age, experience, or expertise. Other forms are a basic level of respect that are shown to everyone at a default. Show respect to your elders, to all people as children of God, and to fellow brothers and sisters of the faith. And also respect yourself. Respect for yourself is shown in upholding your values and morals through your actions, and taking care of yourself. Having self-respect teaches others to also respect you, and it is a very holy quality to have. Respect for others, on the other hand, is displayed through manners. One way you can respect someone is by simply listening to them. Respect reminds you and others of your inherent worth as God's creation. We are all created in the image of God (Genesis 1:27), and it's important to honor this.

My thoughts/ notes:

_____

_____

I have a baseline respect for all people of God's creation and for my fellow brothers in Christ.

What are some specific ways you show people respect?

_____

_____

_____

Can you remember a specific event that occurred in which you showed others that you respect yourself?

_____

_____

_____

DAY 28: PERSEVERANCE

GALATIANS 6:9

"Let's not be weary in doing good, for we will reap in due season, if we don't give up."

Picture yourself as an athlete running a marathon who has tenacity, or the determination to keep going. You choose to run and persevere over being passive. Passivity is the downfall of many men. It can be a catalyst for immorality. An example of this is the story of Aham and his wife Jezebel (1 Kings). Aham wanted the vineyard of his neighbor Naboth, but Naboth wouldn't sell it to him because it was against God's will. Jezebel took matters into her own hands and had Naboth done away with. Aham could have prevented this, but chose to remain passive. Choosing to not persevere to do the right thing can have dire consequences. It can also have consequences for your own personal goals. Don't shrink away from challenges, whether that be pursuing your dream job, your dream girl, or a high moral standard.

My thoughts/ notes:

_____

_____

As a servant of God I have the power to keep going even during times when I don't want to. God always refills my cup so I can take on more, be more, and do more.

The Bible tells us to forget that which is behind us and to look towards the future (Philippians 3:13-14) to persevere. Is there something you have to let go of?

_____

_____

_____

When was one time you persevered against the devil?

_____

_____

_____

DAY 29: REPUTATION

ROMANS 5:3-4

"Not only this, but we also rejoice in our sufferings, knowing that suffering produces perseverance; and perseverance, proven character; and proven character, hope..."

Your reputation precedes you. In other words, people hear about your reputation before they even get to know you personally. As such, it is important to think about how the choices you make today can impact you as a man tomorrow. Whom you choose to associate with and the consequences of your actions can affect you for a long time, for better or worse. It can be hard to remain steadfast in developing a good character, but know that he who remains dedicated during hard times will be blessed (James 1:12). The journey of character development is worth it. All we have is our character, our reputation. It can open doors or close them. And working on developing a godly character can help you spot others of similar character on your walk with Christ.

My thoughts/ notes:

My reputation as a man and as a follower of Jesus Christ is of great importance to me. I guard it to gain God's favor and for my own peace of mind.

Briefly name at least one specific past or current thing that may threaten to hurt your reputation. It could be an emotion, a person, or some other thing that can affect you.

_____

_____

_____

Pray to God to help you with this challenge.

_____

_____

_____

DAY 30: RACE

REVELATION 7:9

"After these things I looked, and behold, a great multitude, which no man could count, out of every nation and of all tribes, peoples, and languages, standing before the throne and before the Lamb..."

The great Kingdom of God is available to all. Black or White, rich or poor, male or female, we are a part of the same human family, united by Christ (Galatians 3:28), and all deserving of compassion and respect as God's creation. Through Christ we can transcend all barriers, for He shows us the way to God and salvation, no matter our background. No group of people are supreme to another. The only supreme being is Christ Himself (Colossians 1:15). Those who believe otherwise are being led astray by the devil. If ever you face discrimination or mistreatment based on skin color or some other trait that is out of your control, know that God sees this injustice (Isaiah 61:8).

My thoughts/ notes:

Black or White I am a part of God's holy family. I worship and acknowledge His divine wisdom which says that we are all equal.

Why do you think God gives us hardships to overcome like mistreatment or racism?

_____

_____

_____

We are called to forgive people who hurt us (Matthew 6:12). If someone hurt you by being prejudiced about your looks, age, background, or anything else, write a brief prayer for them.

_____

_____

_____

DAY 31: AMBITION

COLOSSIANS 3:23

"And whatever you do, work heartily, as for the Lord, and not for men."

Strive to challenge yourself by setting high goals. Worldly goals shouldn't take you further from God though. Ambition does not only involve things like climbing a career ladder, becoming wealthy, or achieving fitness goals. Be ambitious in also striving to become more Christ-like. Success in this spiritual ambition creates a positive feedback loop, begetting success in your other ambitions. God rewards those who have their priorities in the right order and put Him first. Let Him guide your path to greatness as a Black man. He'll give you the tools you need to leave a mark in this world. All of the courage, wisdom, the resolve and vision you need to make your dreams happen will come through Him. As you achieve small successes and later bigger ones, remember to thank the One who got you there.

My thoughts/ notes:

_____

_____

My Lord helps me climb mountains, swim oceans and walk through deserts to meet my goals, praised He be!

What are some current ambitions you have for yourself?

_____

_____

_____

Write a brief prayer asking God to help you bring your ambitions to fruition.

_____

_____

_____

DAY 32: COURAGE

DEUTERONOMY 31:6

"Be strong and courageous. Don't be afraid or scared of them; for Yahweh your God himself is who goes with you. He will not fail you nor forsake you."

God, Jesus and the Holy Spirit watch over you as you go through life. At any time you can look towards the sky and be reminded that you are not alone on your journey. As a young man, you may well encounter moments of change, fear and uncertainty. Be strong and courageous knowing that you have the support and guidance of the Lord (Ephesians 6:10). Like a surfer riding a wave, you may face challenges that threaten to overwhelm you, but with God on your side you can ride out any wave that comes your way. When you face backlash for your Christian beliefs, bravely stand firm and loyal towards God. Bad health and poor sleep can affect your ability to feel courageous, so take care of them. And trust in God to help you embrace the unknown.

My thoughts/ notes:

_____

_____

I am stronger than I know! The Almighty has given me a fighting spirit that I will use in service of the Lord.

Can you think of a feat of courage from a man that you've seen in a movie, on social media, in real life, etc.? Jot it down.

_____

_____

_____

Lots of things can make us brave, such as anger, faith, or even fear of what happens if we're not brave. Think back to times when you have felt courageous. What inspired you?

_____

_____

_____

DAY 33: PRAY MORE

PHILIPPIANS 4:6

"In nothing be anxious, but in everything, by prayer and petition with thanksgiving, let your requests be made known to God."

Prayer paves the way to inner calm and a renewed sense of hope. It is a powerful tool that allows you to communicate with the Almighty at a moment's notice. What a privilege to have! You can always talk to God to find solace and guidance. Instead of dwelling on your worries alone, bring them before Him. Share all of your desires, all of your concerns with humility and with a sincere heart. If you feel unseen or unsupported, remember that there is no better listener than the Lord. Like a loyal friend who offers support and an attentive ear, your prayers are heard by a compassionate and understanding God. Prayer helps you feel lighter, more connected to God, and more receptive to future blessings, so try to pray a lot if you don't already.

My thoughts/ notes:

Father I ask you to hear my prayers and guide me. Let me bask in your divine wisdom and grow in your company Lord.

How often do you pray now? How often would you like to pray?

_____

_____

_____

What are some specific things you want to do to introduce more prayer into your life? This can include scheduled alarms, prayer groups, sticky notes throughout your house to remind you, etc.

_____

_____

_____

DAY 34: MASCULINITY

GENESIS 1:27

"God created man in his own image. In God's image he created him..."

God is infinite. Humans are based on Him, and so they take on infinitely different forms. This includes different forms of masculinity. Though at its core masculinity is based on the ideas previously mentioned (providing, protecting, etc.), it can look different between individuals. Some men show their manliness more through their intellect, and others through athletics. Some are the strong, silent stoic who command respect with few words. Others lead and inspire others with their talkative charm and big personality. Some are "good guys," some are "bad boys". (Bear in mind, the bad boy style of manliness, though still masculine, is not of God). Don't fret if others' displays of manliness differs from your own. Part of being a man is being independent and forging your own God given path in life, regardless of what others think.

My thoughts/ notes:

_____

_____

My masculinity comes from the Almighty. It is a reflection of God's own masculine traits, like strength and headship.

As an individual, how does your God-given masculinity look similar to others' masculinity? How does it differ?

_____

_____

_____

What are a few of the masculine traits that God is known for? What about a few of the feminine traits?

_____

_____

_____

DAY 35: NO PERFECT MAN

PSALM 18:30

"As for God, his way is perfect. Yahweh's word is tried. He is a shield to all those who take refuge in him."

On your path to finding purpose and greatness as a Black man, be forgiving of yourself while still having high standards. There is no such thing as a perfect man. The only exception for this is Jesus. Christ embodies perfection in every aspect of His being. He is and will always be the only example of this, as He is the beginning and the end (Revelation 22:13). Accepting Jesus as your Lord and saviour and aiming for Christ-likeness in your life will make you a respectable man. Though you may fall short of being perfect - like everyone does - God in His everlasting grace looks past this. He gave up His son so you, with all of your imperfections, can live eternally. Always look to the King of kings and as a role model for your own path in life as a man. Let Him inspire you to pursue moral excellence in all that you do.

My thoughts/ notes:

Jesus Christ, my Lord and savior, I promise to study the Gospel to follow closely in your perfect footsteps. Your glory inspires me to grow into a great man!

How great is our God Christ? Take a few sentences to worship Him in all of His glory.

In what specific ways do you think you are not perfect, but can strive to be better for God?

Please feel free to leave a rating or review on Amazon. It would be greatly appreciated!

☆ ☆ ☆ ☆ ☆

Check out **31-Day Bible Study for Black Teens:**

Made in United States
Orlando, FL
04 April 2025